BITTERSWEET

Bittersweet

poems

Natasha Ramoutar

MAWENZI
HOUSE

We acknowledge the support of the Canada Council for the Arts for our publishing program. We also acknowledge support from the Government of Ontario through the Ontario Arts Council, and the support of the Government of Canada through the Canada Book Fund.

Cover design by Sarah Lacasse

Library and Archives Canada Cataloguing in Publication

Title: Bittersweet : poems / Natasha Ramoutar.
Names: Ramoutar, Natasha, 1994- author.
Identifiers: Canadiana (print) 20200310488 | Canadiana (ebook) 20200310518 | ISBN 9781774150207
    (softcover) | ISBN 9781774150214 (EPUB) | ISBN 9781774150221 (PDF)
Classification: LCC PS8635.A46 B58 2020 | DDC C811/.6—dc23

Printed and bound in Canada by Coach House Printing

Mawenzi House Publishers Ltd.
39 Woburn Avenue (B)
Toronto, Ontario M5M 1K5
Canada
www.mawenzihouse.com

for the gyals—
any place with you is home

Contents

bittersweet (adj.)

/ˈbidər͵swēt/

i. knives near-nick heartstrings

ii. and laughter crosscuts tears

iii. you'll feel this most at the end

iv. haunting the back of your tongue

1

Cartography I

Ask me where I come from and I will tell you: from the remnants of melted sugar cubes, from rough grains ripped from stalks, from spiced and saccharine scents, from a sweetness that mixes with cardamom hanging in the air. I come from a line of bittersweet women, women shrewd enough to empty pockets, to upturn kingdoms, to launch ships to war. On a journey long ago, I witnessed the origin point: fields of cane standing tall like soldiers on patrol. But cane is raw; just long stalks, unbridled and wild and free.

Brave New World

The grandmother of my grandmother's grandmother must have arrived on a ship that rolled through tempestuous waves. At least that is what I suspect; where are the faded documents, the sprawling maps, the dog-eared photographs of her journey? The stories I know by heart are not of her; tales of Othello and outcast, of young Miranda all bright-eyed. My father grew up studying Hamlet in grade school. What of spoiled kings, tortured princes, and frigid Danish air was relatable? Grief, maybe. I think of her upon that ship from Denmark, grasping at faeries in the moonlight.

On Reading

My grandmother could neither read nor write,
grew up at home taking care of others so they could go to school
while she cooked dhal and bhagee, pumpkin and roti, scrubbed
    floors till they shined

Words on paper were reduced to symbols, to foreign lines and
    curves
I caught a glimpse of her phone book once—
the same squiggles and curves, lines and edges
of our colonial alphabet in a sequence that only she could
    comprehend

My grandmother could neither read nor write,
but she always read us like open books, our faces like fresh-inked
    pages

I'd watch through glass panels of closed doors as she would cook,
kneading dough the way I needed writing,
putting ingredients in the pot like pen to paper

She would edit the bad words with tea,
sweeten the bitter pages until they were born anew

If I close my eyes, I can sometimes feel
the rough grains of sugar on my tongue once more

Tea Leaves

I shift my tea leaves back and forth,
reading for the past instead of the future

Maybe it's in the bitterness of the Assam leaves,
cultivated to need the touch of sweetness

Maybe it's in the sugar,
grown across baked beaten backs

Maybe it's in the water,
the droplets pooling from the rainy season
into rough-necked bottles

Kali

What ancient part of you stirs when you hear the creak of a door?
What memory reawakens with the soft breath on your skin?
When a stranger grazes your hand, does your heart quicken?

Gaze long in the distance—
do you stare into the dark backward
or avert your eyes?

Moon Children

I wonder if us moon children, softshell crabs that lay on sandy shores where the water lapses to kiss the land, were always destined to be like this. Made more emotional than we are, gaslit to the point of explosions. The root of the word lunacy is Luna, as if the moonlight and the shimmering of the night was the cause of it all, as if flesh and bone, intention and accusation had nothing to do with it.

To those who came before—

I used to look for myself in timelines and dog-eared photos,
trying to trace my body through maps that spanned the world

I want to know how you were all wildfires below monsoon clouds,
flickering flames in tropical rains;

how that one single exhale ignites the light in all of us

Fire

How do you start a fire?

i. Remember that the flame of a match is not that of a wildfire.

ii. Gather the tinder and kindling and firewood.

iii. Set your boundaries with stones—or don't.

iv. Dig your pit as deep as your grave.

v. Make your fire bed and lay in it.

vi. Remember that you are a wildfire.

vii. Remember that the spark begins with a single steady breath.

Tracer

The soot from the ashes of burnt pages
flecks of dried blood like peeled polish
a pathway obscured, long-trodden
If you listen closely to the scratched record
You'll hear a voice below the skipping—
a scream

Bird Song

The words are always on the tip of my tongue,
darting up through the canal of my throat like surging birds,
feathers suspended above acid waves in my stomach

I swallow half-formed questions,
choke back egging sentiments

Tell me again how the nightingale called every night
to a lover who would not decipher her laments,

how the migration passed her by as she sang

Us Diaspora Babies, We Do Not Sleep

ghost babies drawing maps in the margins/
of a place called No Homeland
—KAI CHENG THOM, "diaspora babies"

This boat, it rocks back and forth like a cradle on the Essequibo
    River,
us diaspora babies swathed in red life jackets,
the steady shifting trying to lull us to dream.

Us diaspora daughters,
those who can lap lakes, wade water,
us dewy children
trying to navigate the ocean
The way our mothers could not.

This boat, it rocks back and forth like a cradle on the Essequibo
    River,
just as it does along the Cuyuni and the Demerara,
the Pomeroon and the Mazaruni.
I wonder if this water flows home,
if the river has ever made its way to the Rouge,
met up lapping like the forgotten siblings they are.

This boat tries to comfort,
but us diaspora babies,
we do not sleep—
only dream with eyes wide open,
grasping at the water of our homelands,
droplets slipping through our fingers with each midsummer
    breeze.

Us diaspora daughters,
listening to our parents' stories of the golden era
of a far off youth.

We know of home through photographs and UN reports,
but what of seeing with our own eyes?
What of divided states of being?

What of us diaspora babies,
us diaspora daughters,
exiled before birth?

Time II

What is time but a set of coincidences, of stars and planets falling in line, of weighty gravities that pulls us like rising tides, of undertows dragging us towards that which beckons, of seized opportunities, conjured from dusty books, of constellations twinkling like eyes as we move?

Many Tongues

I do not speak
in my mother's tongue of exasperated sighs and soft laughs,
those noises that sit side to slight smiles

I do not speak
the dialect of my grandmother,
struggling to imitate her voice as she says
yuh tek yuh eyes and pass me

I do not speak
the words of those women before my grandmother
from some long lost homeland across oceans

I try to wrap my mouth
around the stretched vowels of the word *jaan;*

come up empty
and gasping
every time

Translation by Sound

एक-ing like a long lost bird, like a दो from her mother,
like the young तीन with a half-mended heart |

चार your venison deep red,
mix the blood with पांच
while छ-tting among your neighbours |

I once सात at the edge of the world |

The आठ-or always thinks they know what's best for नौ ||

Savasana | *Corpse Pose*

Lay flat on your back in savasana with your eyes closed. Loosen every knotted tension in the length of your neck, in the curves of your jaw, in the tug of disbelief in your mind. Take a moment to survey your body, the brownness of your skin, the thickness of your hair. Realize that you are the only one like this in the room. Let the thought pass. Allow your breath to guide your practice, your belly rising on each inhale and sinking with each exhale. Turn your palms upward to the sky like a prayer. Pretend that your spirit recognizes the sanskrit at the end of class. Whisper a half-hearted "namaste." When are you ready, open your eyes.

Ink

What I tell my sister: *I want a tattoo.*
What I don't tell her: *I want flowers to bloom from the corners of my body, and vines to ride up and down my legs like some sort of new age Poison Ivy. I want moons and waves and forests. I want to be a landscape.*

What she tells me: *You'd have to hide it.*
What she doesn't tell me: *It is shameful to ink your body. Keep your surface plain and unaltered. Refrain from piercing dipped needles through your skin.*

What I tell her (smirk): *Grandma has a tattoo.*
What I do not tell her: *Grandma must have gotten her tattoo very young, younger than me, because it is faded and stretches in the folds of her skin.*

What she tells me (laugh): *Grandma didn't have a choice.*
What she does not tell me: *Our grandmother, tender and young, must have been branded like an animal.*

What I don't tell my sister: *Maybe I am already inked, a darkness that passes beneath the skin, from generation to generation.*

Coda

Creeping along my skin and nipping at muscle,
trying to enter through open pores
Coding fear and anger into the body,
criminalizing the voice falls on closed ears

Where is the micro in your aggression?

Navigator

"I've never heard of Guyana," he says.
I spin the globe to our hemisphere,
place the magnifying glass
above the cluster of islands
and jagged mainland,
above rough shores of the Caribbean,
and tell him,
"Look upon gold."
He leans close to gaze,
caresses the embossed land with the
tip of his finger.

This Be the Verse

After Philip Larkin

White men have wine game but no whine game

Port Royal

"The Caribbean Sea was ruled by white men."

That isn't incorrect;
white noise drowns us out.

But we were always there,
along the docks,
amidst the granules of sand,
as serpents below the waves.

There were more Tia Dalmas in every port;
                    more Calypsos to sway the sea.

Atlantis

As if El Dorado wasn't just a rum,
As if mermaids waited at seaports

Window-seated in the airplane,
I see the sea's surface ripple and break,
the tip of a tail plunging back towards its depths

Aeroplane

There is a moment just above Port of Spain where the plane dips,

a rising feeling of weightlessness

Outside the window, the wing bisects the world—
above, a sliver of the moon hung like a hangnail;
below, the city lights like a field of stars

Rock Bottom

I fish hooked fingers
into near-dry ponds

and break
sheet reflections

Watching skin
long-baked in the sun,

I strain for
past present
in the image of myself

There are no time lines
on my palm,

only skin and bone and flesh

Somewhere in this pond
there is a buried lineage,

a sunken ship
from an unfamiliar home

Parts & Labours

Can we import our homeland,
ship it across waters in Wamara-wood barrels?

Does the weight of our ancestors bob
like Peardrax bottles in waves?

Should we spend weekends sorting through sugarcane
or searching for hassa with perfect sets of scales?

Is there a way to fry accents into our doubles?
To fold in fetes into our dough?

Tell me, please—

have you found out which of the twelve labours
will give us our missing parts?

Earth

Not   quite   like
    the   earth,
                    p u l l e d   from   their
                    native soil,
        repotted,
                replanted,
                        transplanted to a new
                        environment   that
    didn't   quite   take,
            nipped   root
            s
    encroached   by   the   local
                floral

        (encroaching on local flora? as experts report),

    roots   too   foreign   for
                    here
            but   too   tender   for
        the   spoiled   soil   of
                    home,
a little one
        who   eventually   stayed   with   roots
    reaching   for   the
                    centre of the earth,   molten   and
                engulfing,
    that   couldn't   shake   the feeling of   not
            belonging,   even   after
            generations   and generations.

East

Where the wind's eye rested,
launched seeds to cross-pollinate,
to grow in cracks in cement
between the basketball nets and rusty swing sets,
all of us sea glass in the playground sand

Where you can trim the stem,
and the roots grow unruly
or when you cut the glass,
it magnifies the heat

Someone once told me:
resilience is born of pain and desire

We reach for the sun, uprising

Meadowvale

These streets
are yours. They
have always
been yours,
with the dark
cracks running
up like veins
along the aged
cement. With
the blinking
bulbs keeping
you in their line
of sight. The air
that rises off the
sewer lids like a
hot breath. The
dandelions that
sprout between
the sidewalk and
the pot-holed
road.

198

This poem was waiting for the bus,
watching raindrops race along panes

of the bus shelter, composing itself
to the steady beat of the downpour.

·After 50 minutes it began to walk,
the deluge a refuge

from the roughness of rouge,
each drop a nonstop pop of ideas,

orbs of light to reunite a wavering line of sight.
When this poem arrived home it shed

its skin, folded every metaphor
into its closet, tucked itself in and

dreamed of a homebound bus.

Time III

What is time but stolen glances beyond straight-lined
desks and lockers across the hall, that line of sight
through the dirty RT window as the train pulls into
Kennedy Station, the slight nod of acknowledgement,
a hint of a smile before parting ways again?

Travellers

Ours is a city of travellers,
                    each of us bundled up in the winter,
waterproof boots and jackets, lined hoods,
   puffed like marshmellows on the packed streetcar.

We dart around the city like mice to a mousehole,
   leaving nothing but melted footprints as evidence.

Brimley, All the Way South

Head northeast toward Military Trail, away from these concrete towers, superimposed over the spiralling paths in the Valley. 230 m

Turn left onto Military Trail, noting the way the road is chaotic, that the intersection does not line up cleanly. 130 m

Turn left onto Ellesmere Rd to escape this chaos. 450 m

Turn left onto Morningside Ave. Feel your spirit rise and fall with the natural hills. 1.7 km

Turn right onto Kingston Rd. As you pass the motels, remember, this was the arterial pathway into the heart of the city. 7.2 km

Turn left onto Brimley Rd. Take Brimley all the way south to the place where the water meets the land. 1.3 km

Continue onto Bluffers Park. Remember that Elizabeth Simcoe renamed this place, renamed a land long-named. 110 m

Turn right to stay on Bluffers Park. Think about how we are neither water nor rocks, just zebra mussels that cling to one another, swaying with the waves. Think about how we don't deserve this land. 350 m

Turn right. Destination will be on the right, waiting.

All Inclusive

Location
Only where waves reach white-sand beaches,
places we can dub nirvana

Duration
Six days of escaping,
six days of imposing

Arrival
You can't see anything from inside the hotel walls,
a fortress in the sandy land of paradise,
another monument to those who never
conjured fully-formed thoughts of this place

Departure
Our planes land in Pearson at the same time,
the haphazard lines converging
you with your neck pillow and sweatpants,
and us garbed in black, as if at a funeral

jumbie (noun)

/jəmbē/

i. The word jumbie is a jumbie in itself: a coffin with no body, an urn with ashes scattered

ii. The dead air of the early morning, in which we wake to grasp at empty shadows

iii. A memory of a long faded memory of our grandparents in dirt streets below the moon beams

iv. The buzz of mosquitos as they come and go like ghosts

Bloody Mary

Lightbulbs flickered as we chanted, our eyes fixated on our own shadow-haired reflections. We only ever saw ourselves, ghosts washed pale in the fluorescent beams.

Our parents used to tell us, *Walk in the house backwards or the jumbies will follow you in.* Now grown, we leave the doors open; stand in the doorway, waiting to hear a different ghost story.

Sweet Like Sugar

My blood must be cane juice with all these mosquito bites,
the way the skin puckers, pursed and red as though waiting for a
  kiss.

Fresh blood, calls one.

Foreign blood, another.

Swell

When we arrive in Guyana,
my mother's feet swell from the sweltering heat,

as if our bodies do not know this country's fire
courses through our veins,

as if it has forgotten that my mother is from this soil,
that her skin was scrubbed with its sugar,

that the heat is a long lost friend welcoming her home

Air

Hot and sticky and encompassing,
silence that is stagnant and still,
everything at once that is nothing
at all, that is there that is not
there, the space in the fold of the
sheets stamped with their shape,
a spectre that leans over my
shoulder breathing, asking once
more only to disappear when I
turn to look.

Kaiteur

It exists
on a frayed embroidered map,
where I pulled at gold threads,
searching for the first stitch.

We trail over roots and rocks next to the unbarred water,
until we reach Kaiteur, *Kai's house.*
Long stalks brush my cheeks,
eyes peeled for poisonous golden toads, a jolt between leaves,
for bushmaster serpents and rainbow boas blending with
    overgrown roots.
I expected
to find Kai within these running waters,
but he is not mine to find.
Instead I grip the granular edge.

Why did you sacrifice yourself?
What did Makonaima say to you?
Had others done the same
when boats docked on these sandy shores?

This place is often called the Land of Six People;
Perhaps five of us are visitors.

Gold

A daughter is a visitor in her father's home.

My future wedding band, although I prefer silver. The mangalsutra, beads clinging to the throat. Our lineage, woven together in a solid gold strand. A mother's heart when she gives her daughter away. This moment, and every moment thereafter.

My First Love

was *kathak*, was trying to count *taal* in 16 beats, was watching senior dancers spotlighted like item girls, was each tabla beat, was my dance teacher, was *jhaptaal* and *sargam*, was trying to pleat the dupattas neatly, was channeling my inner Aishwarya Rai, was running out of bobby pins, was draping heavy fabric along the length of my body, was scarlet and gold like the air during *holi*, was the moment my heart stuttered on that last *sam* at the end of the set.

Woods and Water

When the bass hits at Danforth Hall,
it starts in the souls of my feet,
shimmies up slender spine grooves,
spreads through my ribs to cup my heart like a hug
as though each soundwave is an ocean in itself,
as though each ripple reminds us that
we were all seachildren,
salty and dribbling,
murmuring wishes to the open air

Beached

Echo Beach is a womb
where we premature sea turtles are buried
and for a moment, I think I'm getting soft with salty tears,
but our moon-crescented shells were always waiting
for these lyrics and we lean our sunbaked bodies up to the barrier,
sweat-caked shoulders pressed together and I feel the bass
    sprinting
upwards past my heart, rumbling in the throat like words held by
    closed lips,
begging to crack the shell and embrace the sky
and when the harmonies start,
I think for a moment that I am 16 again:
girls like sisters whispering past dark,
spread across the basement floor under a sea of comforters,
our laughter weaving into one collective prayer

Like Makeshift Crowns

Could we speak about joy for once?
About July nights by the lake,
about dripping marshmallows
over the rising smoke of the bonfire,
about laughter that filled our bodies,
got caught in our throats as coughs
in our eyes as tears?

Of the five of us tripping over stray branches in the Rouge,
of toes pressed in the sand around a withering fire,
of stretched nights squeezed
in a McDonald's booth meant for four,
of us comforter-wrapped slugs on worn basement carpet,
hair piled atop our heads
like makeshift crowns.

Joy is not a whispered story
but a wailing manifesto:
of rampant roots reaching for the heavens,
of tides pulled to shore by a wanton moon,
of flecks of dried ketchup painting the table,
of the weathered stars winking at us
through the 4-by-6 window.

We drive out,
under the vast night sky,
looking up at the moon through the sunroof,
the bass from the stereo shaking the frame of the car,
as if it's laughing.

Could we speak about dreams?
About us making a wish on the star falling into the lake,
for more nights like this,
where we line up along the rocks,
toes grazing the water,
our giggles rising with the tide as if to say,
I am here.

Cartography II

Were we, us women, ever friends before? Was there ever a time where we didn't raise Hell and its demons with our voices? I come from women whose voices herd clouds and conjure storms, whose shrieks command thunder and eyes wield lightning. I quake like the earth, tremors from my toes upward. I think of my sister, the water rippling from the vibrato.

Water

Cool and slight, sometimes a slight ripple

Beneath the moon, the fish swim,
bubbles breaking the surface of the still water

The moon called to me four times—
on the fifth I answer
hello

Edge into the ocean step by step
Until my hair reaches wildly for the surface
a wave

Eternal Summer

It begins with a single note;
—one pluck of a guitar string,
—a single tabla beat,
—the giggle of the steel pan

The rhythm only moves forward
winding through the grass,
stops briefly to gaze at the clouds,
leaps through the windows of houses

I follow the muddy footprints,
skipping like stones across rippled water

When I reach the shore, I gaze towards the sun,
grin defiant as an imp

And We Got Older

People grow up by accident, while playing tag and tripping over roots, licking ice cream that drips down our arms, smuggling candy into theatres, only to look up and see our faces on the screen like a sigh.

Famous Players

The hub of life   is dead today.
—ADRIAN DE LEON, "Scarborough Centre"

Wayfaring wanderers among the aisles of clothing,

we'd parade in suits in the empty changerooms,

hold cheap plastic pearls up to our ears in the mirrors

until we were chased away.
Vagabonds with stray loonies amidst our pocket lint, smuggling chocolates

into an uninhabited theatre. We clutched hands

below the kernels of popcorn, lips smeared with melted butter as the screen filled our eyes with promises

that touched the centre of us,

childish drifters looking for life in an abandoned mausoleum.

The Alchemists

The scrolls and maps drape every surface,
      pinned to the walls,
      hanging over chairs
      in this dimly lit lab.
We're trying to find immortality,
      as if time could heal our pain.
My gaze rests on the beaker,
      the smoke rising in puffs,
      wheezing last
         breaths away.
We turn lead into gold,
      as if gold isn't poison itself.

Atlas Hugged

I waver between
wanting to hold the world
and wanting the world to hold me

The History of Movement

Of jewel-encrusted jhoomars
dripping below courtesans' hairlines

Of sufi dancers' endless whirling,
pearl-white skirts flaring in devotion

Every spin is making magic with your feet

Rewind

What if time did not move forwards, but backwards?
We could place the pencil in the circle of the
cassette, spin the translucent film counterclockwise
until the hours became ours again, until we could
hold that second in cupped hands, gazing at it like a
glimmering snowglobe caught in the light.

Tandem

We sit tandem to the mandem, us gyaldem who stem from same soil but branch for shade, both given and thrown, for those who are blem from the AM to the PM, us women who care too much for them.

Whose Mans?

Mans, mandem, sweetermans, bodman, wasteman,
and starboys, blazing pinpricks in the celestial sphere

Howl

We were watching stars that night in the Rouge,

the moonbeams reaching for our skin through the canopy of trees
the river trickled softly, the crickets in full chorus throughout the
  grass

Across the bank, something shifted

My breath caught in my throat as a wavering howl rang out
A lone coyote emerged, its mouth tight

I turned back to see you:
lips parted, teeth bared, eyes yellow as the moon

Rouge Rocks

Thise rokkes sleen myn herte for the feere.
—DORIGEN, *The Franklin's Tale*

Those shaded rocks stacked sitting straight side slightly tilted,
crooked like a husband who tries his wife right,
curved like a mistress with narrow straight words,
warped like the lover who leaves footsteps in your foyer
folded with their scent,
an illusion as these tender rouge rocks

Murmuring of Starlings

When stars fall, they fall slowly.
They hover, peering at wayward wishes
sent out into the night sky.
They pause to shake off dreams,
attracted like magic.
When they land, they nestle close together;
share tales of reveries of yesteryear.

sweetermans (noun)

/swētərmans/

i. These sons want to be sweetermans, to cause cavities with one gaze, race hearts with a graze, for each smacking of lips to leave grainy remnants as reminders

ii. Our mothers want their sons to be sweeter mans, kind and loving, to draw flies to honey, nourish their loves bathing in sugary syrup

Sweetened Words

Can you pick the sugar from the salt?

Salt

used to preserve youth in the years 2016-20XX. They retreated into the briny water of themselves, became tough like strips of cured fish, tightened their lids and sat in dark, cool cellars. Pour salt in all their wounds and watch them laugh.

Dead Watch

Stuck in some sort of adolescence, always digging up graves to watch ghosts of past selves. The empty sockets of the skeletons gaze up dripping dirt, their hands clutching 12 as though the past is the only time worth holding.

Photograph

They would have sat for hours as the imprint burned into the paper, the sepia treatment flattening the layers of their shaded skin, their mouths in tight lines because smiles were too laborious to keep. A pristine rectangle taunts me in the photo album, the only white space in the brown-smudged collection. I imagine flipping the lost image over, smoothing my hand over the worn ink on the back, waiting to see if the numbers would shift as unruly spirits in the origin point:

1838

Heat

The way it feels after
the rains, below the
heavy-lidded   palm
trees, the way it rests
on my shoulders like
the touch of an old
confidant passing by.

Melting Pot

Ingredients:

> 2 cups of water
>
> 1 cup of rice
>
> 3 dreams (crushed)
>
> 2 tablespoon of silence
>
> ½ teaspoon of submissiveness

Directions

1. Enter the pot.

2. Watch the water slowly increase to a boil. Break the rising bubbles with your fingertips.

3. Resist the lightning running through your legs, the instinctive knee jerk to launch yourself out.

4. Close your eyes. Simmer quietly.

5. Try to piece together the dreams swirling between the uncooked grains.

6. Avoid the falling salt, the black pepper to add a *kick*.

7. Never add your own flavours. They're not a good fit.

Suture

It tears at stuttering hearts
and gasping lungs,
leaves gashes that I try
to suture again and again

but these wounds swell and burst
beneath the thread

Egg Shells

How many of our parents
walked on cracked egg shells to raise us?
Minds thick yolked from ghost-white skulls,
their internal screams silently reverberating
against paper thin walls.
Every irritable snap, sleepless night,
empty feeling resting in the belly—ignored.

Nothing a cup of tea can't fix,
they must have reassured themselves,
some limacool and vicks.

Time I

What is time but a series of rivers flowing
in every direction, crossing and weaving
to form a net that catches you, holds you
and—when nothing else will—mends you
whole in a dream-sleep?

Blue Prints

I lay my blueprints down like an architect,

letters touching grid top and bottom,
curving up into smiles,
laying straight like a walking path,

guiding eyes to string sounds into lines,
into patterns, into geometrics

building structures from calligraphy,
roofs to keep the poems dry,

a place to house my smudged navy ink

sketching stories by fireplaces,
the smoke imprints on my skin and hair
like a now-found lover

Unravel

How do you unravel a history of trauma, that which is woven
  within you?

  Tug at each thread and watch yourself bared, that glimmering red
                                                              flesh.

How do you weave long-scorched ends in with the new?

                      Smooth the ends with coconut oil. It comes together
                                                                slowly.

Acknowledgements

The first poem I ever wrote for this collection—before I could even fathom writing a collection— was "Cartography I." Thank you to Hawa Y. Mire, who delivered the writing workshop at the University of Toronto Scarborough (UTSC)'s Women & Trans Centre Conference that started this all. I always had a hard time writing about concepts of "homeland." Your workshop gave me the tools I was missing. I am so grateful.

To the incredible luminaries Carrianne Leung, Catherine Hernandez, and David Chariandy, thank you for making me brave. Your works, kindness, and support give me the confidence to continue writing my hometown onto the page.

I have so much love for RISE, Wave, The Group Project, Scarborough Arts, and so many other community organizations and collectives doing the work in Scarborough and proving there is space for all of us. Thank you as well to BAM and Up From the Roots for allowing me to test out a few of these poems on the open mic, and for always bringing the most moving work to the stage.

I gratefully acknowledge the financial support of Ontario Arts Council and Toronto Arts Council. Thank you to the League of Canadian Poets' *Poetry Pause*, Metatron's *#micrometa*, *Living Hyphen*, *Contemporary Verse 2*, *Room Magazine*, and Scarborough Arts' *Big Art Book* for featuring earlier versions of these poems.

Thank you to my teachers at West Hill CI who made me fall in love with literature: Ms. Sengupta, Ms. MacDonell, Ms. Hicks, and Mr. Cohen. Ms. MacDonell, thank you for reassuring me that wanting to be a writer wasn't some bizarre, unattainable dream. Almost a decade later, I still think about that conversation often.

Thank you to Professors Daniel Scott Tysdal and Andrew

Westoll for your care and attention to my creative writing. Thank you as well to Professors Kara Gaston and Marjorie Rubright whose courses allowed me to dive deep into language.

Writing is often made out to be a solitary practice, but my writing only exists within a community of others. Thank you to Justine Abigail Yu and everyone in the pages of Living Hyphen for resonating with my experiences. Thank you to the kindest mentors and sweetest cohort at the Banff Centre as I edited these poems while I was supposed to be writing short fiction. Thank you to Jael Richardson, Amanda Leduc, and the whole team at the Festival of Literary Diversity (FOLD) for introducing me to a plethora of incredible authors. When I found the FOLD, I felt like I had been waiting my whole life to find these writers.

Thank you to scholar Ryan Persadie. I'm so glad our paths crossed during that academic conference at Ryerson University. I'm grateful for the way you helped reshape the way I think about my relationship to the Caribbean and South Asia.

I owe my mentor Sheniz Janmohamed an immense and immeasurable number of thank yous. Thank you for helping me fine-tune every single poem in this collection. Thank you for having honest discussions with me about the business side of publishing. Thank you for that pep talk years ago at the FOLD when I told you that I had been rejected from every MFA program I applied to. And lastly, thank you for making me, a poet with no "formal," institutionally-recognized poetry training, believe that this collection was something substantial.

Thank you to Nurjehan Aziz and the team at Mawenzi House for taking a chance on this collection. I am touched by your care of my work. Thank you to the brilliant Sarah Lacasse for designing the cover of this book.

To my Scarborough writers Leanne Toshiko Simpson, Adrian De Leon, Oubah Osman, Chelsea La Vecchia and Téa Mutonji— I am so deeply moved by your works. I look forward to the day when I can line all of the spines of our books up on my bookshelf. Thank you for your love and support and feedback and encouragement.

Thank you to Kevin Ramroop for being a sounding board for so many of these poems. Thank you to Noor Khan, whose projects consistently show me what true artistic community work looks like. And of course, thank you to Adrian De Leon. There are not enough words to express how grateful I am for your friendship and collaboration. To quote you, "let's keep writing this story."

To the gyals (Mackenzie Dawson, Hiba Hussain, Sarah Lacasse, and Miranda Ramnarayan), Adrian Agrippa and Pirouz Salari—thank you for making this place home. There are so many traces of all of you in these poems, from "Like Makeshift Crowns" to "Meadowvale" to "Murmuring of Starlings."

Dearest Ling Lam and Daniela Spagnuolo, thank you for always being in my corner and cheering me on.

Thank you to my parents and my sisters, always.

And lastly to you, the reader. Thank you for picking this book up. I hope something in this collection made you feel ways.